MAD JACK BOOKS

YO YO

Written by Mike Knowles
Illustrated by David Mostyn

HENDERSON

An imprint of DK Publishing, Inc.
Copyright © 1996 Dorling Kindersley Ltd.

Mad Jack's History of the Yo-Yo

The first recorded yo-yo was this one...

It was seen in a cave drawing made by a prehistoric man (or woman). Scientists believe that the drawing is about 10,000 years old, give or take a day or two.

Look at the drawing. It shows that the first yo-yo was squarish in shape. This proves that the yo-yo was made before the wheel was invented. Scientists think the prehistoric yo-yo was carved out of solid rock and was probably as heavy as a large sack of Idaho potatoes.

Here's a little experiment you can try...

Get a sack of Idaho potatoes and tie a string around it. Now use it like a yo-yo. It will prove four things:

1 Prehistoric man wasn't very bright.

2 Prehistoric man was VERY strong.

3 A sack of Idaho potatoes makes a very bad yo-yo.

4 You shouldn't do everything people tell you.

That was a just a joke. Actually it was the ancient Chinese who invented the yo-yo. They did it at about the same time as they invented gunpowder. It was a disastrous mixture....

Man blows himself up with yo-yo

SO MUCH FOR THE HISTORY OF THE YO-YO! TIME FOR A VOYAGE OF DISCOVERY...

How
Does

Who cares?

Let's face it, you don't need to know how a yo-yo works to use one. In which case you might be wondering why I put this part in.

Here's the reason....

There's a certain group of people out there. I call them *destructive* people. They're pretty strange. You give them a yo-yo and they can't resist the temptation to pull it apart just to see how it works.

You've heard the expression, "Curiosity killed the cat"? Well, take my word for it, it doesn't do much for yo-yos, either.

Sensible people know that if you take your yo-yo apart, you won't be able to put it back together again. Which means you're going to look pretty stupid, right? I mean, try explaining that to your parents! And why bother in the first place? After all, there's nothing complicated about a yo-yo. But, because some people are just plain nosy, I decided to explain in order to satisfy their insatiable curiosity.

It work?

Here's a yo-yo I took apart. You'll see it's made up of three parts....

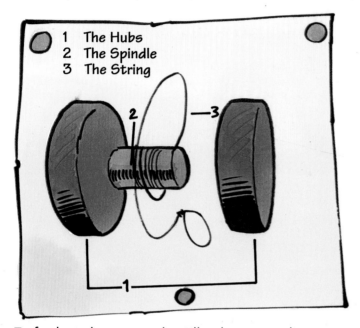

1   The Hubs
2   The Spindle
3   The String

To find out how it works, I'll ask our resident scientist, Sir Isaac Newton. He's been practicing with it....

Actually, the yo-yo is a bit like someone doing a bungee jump. You can demonstrate the principle with this little experiment: just let the yo-yo drop and when it reaches the bottom of the string, keep your hand perfectly still.

This is what should happen....

1 The yo-yo falls, unwinding the string from the spindle.

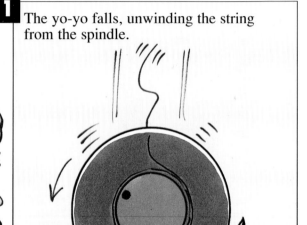

2 When it reaches the bottom, the weight of the yo-yo causes the string to stretch.

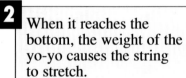

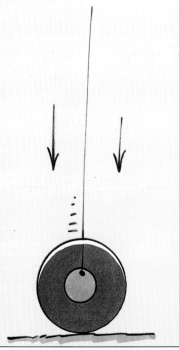

3 The string contracts, sending the yo-yo back up.

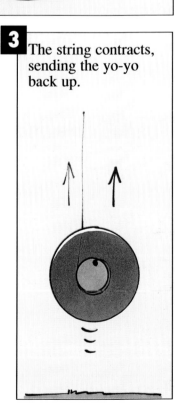

4 As the yo-yo turns, it starts to wind the string back on the spindle.

9

Ah! But there's a problem, right?

The problem is that the yo-yo didn't bounce all the way back up to the top. That's because the string didn't stretch very far. So what you have to do is help it along. Which brings us to the...

EXCITING STUFF

DO NOT OPEN UNTIL PAGE 10

SAFE
Yo-Yoing

Well, *nearly* to the exciting stuff. First of all – take heed!

Never…*ever*…swing your yo-yo around like this:

10

If there's someone near you, it can hit them on the head. *This is painful.* Take my advice: clobbering someone with a lump of wood or plastic swinging around at 60 mph is *not* the best way to make friends with them.

Worse still…

it could damage your beloved yo-yo!

Even if there's no one around, the string could break. When that happens, your harmless little yo-yo will turn into a misguided missile that could break a window or blind the cat.

Yes, I know. Right now you're probably getting impatient. You're saying, "Enough of this nonsense! Who cares about the history of the yo-yo or how it works. Let's get down to some serious business."

Yo-yoing can be a hazard to your health.

not!

The Roll Start

This one needs a bit of practice.

1 Get down on your knees.

2 Pray. No…that was a joke. Place the yo-yo upright on the ground in front of you. The string must be pointing toward you.

3 Pull the string gently and the yo-yo will start rolling toward you. As it does, the string will wrap itself around the spindle.

4 Once the yo-yo reaches the halfway point, stand up and raise it into the air. It will now do a Bungee.

3 Bow when your friends applaud.

4 Continue your trick.

The Roll Start (Version 2)

This one's a bit more difficult.

1 Kneel down and place the yo-yo upright on the ground close to you. This time the string should be pointing away from you.

2 Make sure that part of the string lies straight on the ground.

3 Flick the yo-yo lightly with your finger and make it roll along the string.

4 Stand up, raise the yo-yo into the air, and go into a Bungee.

The Jump Start

This one is even harder.

1 Wait until the yo-yo stops moving.

2 Now jerk the string up and down so that the yo-yo begins to bounce. This is the tricky part. The key is to build up a nice, steady rhythm – not too much and not too little.

3 The idea is to get the yo-yo bouncing up and down so that the string begins to wrap itself around the spindle. You'll need to experiment to get the right amount of bounce. Like I said – these tricks need a lot of practice.

4 If you keep the yo-yo bouncing until there's enough wrapped around the spindle, it will start to roll up and down the string.

5 Once it starts to roll up and down the string, you can start doing a Bungee.

20

The Kick Start

Brrrrmmmm! Brrrrmmmm! Get out that black leather jacket and put some grease in your hair! While doing this last trick start, you can imagine that your yo-yo has turned into a Harley-Davidson motorcycle.

1 Rest the yo-yo upright on the floor, keeping the string slack.

2 Place the toe of your shoe on top of the yo-yo.

3 Now press down with your foot. The idea is to make the yo-yo spin backward. You'll be able to feel it move under your foot. And as it spins, it begins to wind the string around the spindle. Knowing how hard to press takes practice.

4 When you think there's enough string around the spindle, raise the yo-yo up. If the start's been done correctly, the yo-yo should roll up and down enough for you to do a Bungee.

NOW THAT YOU CAN GET YOURSELF OUT OF TROUBLE, WE CAN GO ON TO DO SOME TRICKS....

EASY

Ta-daaa! You're about to do your first trick! It's called "High Diver."

1 Hold the yo-yo firmly in the palm of your hand.

2 Now turn your hand over so that your palm is facing up.

3 Flip the yo-yo over the front of your hand and do a Bungee.

4 As the yo-yo comes back up, turn your hand over to catch it.

5 That wasn't very difficult, was it? Actually, it's a lot more fun when you do it over water (or in the tub). Then you can see the splash as it lands. High Diver is a good trick to start off with because it's so easy to learn. Any fool can do it – even me.

WELL...ER...I CAN DO IT MOST OF THE TIME.

TRICKS

TRIPPING YOUR YO-YO

Now concentrate, everyone, because you won't be able to progress far into yo-yotology until you've mastered the art of making your yo-yo "trip."

Throw your yo-yo into a High Diver. As it hits the bottom, try to soften the final bump before it spins back up. With practice, this should "trip" the yo-yo out of rhythm and leave it spinning merrily away at the bottom like a wheel on an axle. Trip it up again with a slight jolt, and it will wind itself back up to your hand.

If your yo-yo isn't easily tripped, check the spindle. The loop of string around it needs to be just right. If it's too tight, it won't trip. Too loose, and it will trip up forever and not rewind itself. To loosen a tight knot, let the yo-yo hang gently at the end of its string for a moment. Loosen up and unwind, man....

TICK TOCK

OK, let's move on to the next trick.
Surprise, surprise, it's supposed to copy
the movement of the pendulum on a
grandfather clock. (Or even a grand-
mother clock, come to think of it.)

1 Start with a Bungee straight down.

2 Do your next Bungee at an angle, like this.

3 Now do your third Bungee straight down.

4 Then do the fourth Bungee at an angle in the opposite direction of number two.

Repeat 1, 2, 3, and 4 until you build up a nice rhythm.
It takes some concentration, so stick with it. That's the
other thing you have to develop. You have to develop
the art of concentration.

Remember – all the skill in the world is no good if you can't concentrate.

As you advance with your "tripping" techniques, attempt this trick.

1 Hold your arm as though you were going to snap your fingers by your ear. High Dive your yo-yo out to one side. Trip it as it is fully extended.

2 Now swing your tripping yo-yo down in front of you, following the path of a pendulum, out to the other side.

3 As it reaches horizontal, flick it out of its trip, and let it whizz back in to your hand. Amazing.

Walking The Dog

LET'S WALK...

1 Do a few High Divers. When you're feeling confident, trip the yo-yo so it spins.

2 Gently lower the yo-yo onto the ground and it should start rolling.

3 Trip the yo-yo up and continue doing your Bungees.

Nothing to it, right? OK, get a bucket of water. Now let's see if you can make the yo-yo walk over that. Once you've done that, you can move on to the difficult parts....

Before it gets too TRICKY...

Here are some trickster tips for tricky tricks.

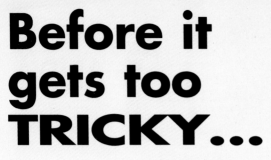

- These tricks need lots of practice, so be prepared to put some time aside each day.

- It can be anything from ten minutes to an hour, depending on how dedicated you are. Call it your practice session. And stick to it.

- You're bound to make mistakes, so you'll also need a lot of patience. If you don't get it right the first time, keep trying.

- Never...ever...lose your temper and chuck your yo-yo away. Yo-yos have feelings, too. So do people – especially if your yo-yo hits them!

- Just remember: if you keep at it long enough, it will come in the end. (Even if it does take years!)

Up AND OVER

Another trick in which you trip up your yo-yo.

1 Bungee down and trip the yo-yo at the bottom.

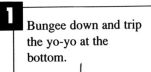

2 With the yo-yo tripping merrily on its own, lift your hand up to your ear.

3 Move your elbow in front of the string (keep the yo-yo still, tripping all the while).

4 Now drop your hand forward and lift your elbow. The jerk should trip your yo-yo out of its spin and unwind itself over your shoulder. Simple? Well, it's easier to do than to describe.

Backflip

1 Throw your yo-yo out to the side, like you did in "Tick Tock." Trip it at the end.

2 Let it swing down again like a pendulum.

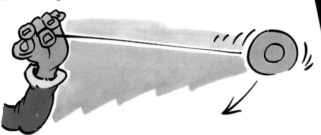

3 As it reaches the other horizontal, clasp the string with your finger and thumb. Don't jerk the yo-yo out of its tripping mode.

4 Your yo-yo should spin around and around as if it is doing a series of backflips. Don't get your fingers tangled in the string!

5 Let go of the string as the yo-yo loses momentum. Trip it out of its spin and Bungee it back up.

Now I'm putting my mortar-board on again. That's 'cause we're about to get into some highly technical stuff. It would help if you graduated Phi Beta Kappa in physics from a top university. Any top university will do, I'm not fussy.

YOU DIDN'T?

Ah, shame on you. I guess you'll just have to do the best you can.

Here we go: in some of these tricks I'll be using what we experts call the "Angled Bungee." So what's an Angled Bungee? Well, there are two basic Bungee types:

THE PERPENDICULAR BUNGEE

Funnily enough, it goes straight down.

THE ANGLED BUNGEE

Surprise – this goes off at an angle. It can be expressed by the square root of the right-angled triangle; where the hypotenuse of the angular momentum is a function of the total area squared by mass times the distance to the Moon, which must be made out of green cheese.

Alternatively, you could just hold the yo-yo in your palm, wrist bent so that your palm faces backward, and fling the yo-yo forward and out. Vary the angle as you see fit – this "shot" can hurtle straight forward or out and down.

MAD JACK'S
SAFETY CODE

When throwing your yo-yo out at an angle, always make sure that there's plenty of empty space around you. Or else this might happen:

33

All clear? Good. Now we can go on to the first difficult trick....

Around

This one's pretty easy (for a difficult one). And there are various songs to sing while practicing:
"Been around the world...la la la."

1 Start with an Angled Bungee and trip your yo-yo at the end.

2 Still tripping, swing the yo-yo out at an angle so that it does a complete circle. (As you can see, the circle goes around the front and back of your hand.)

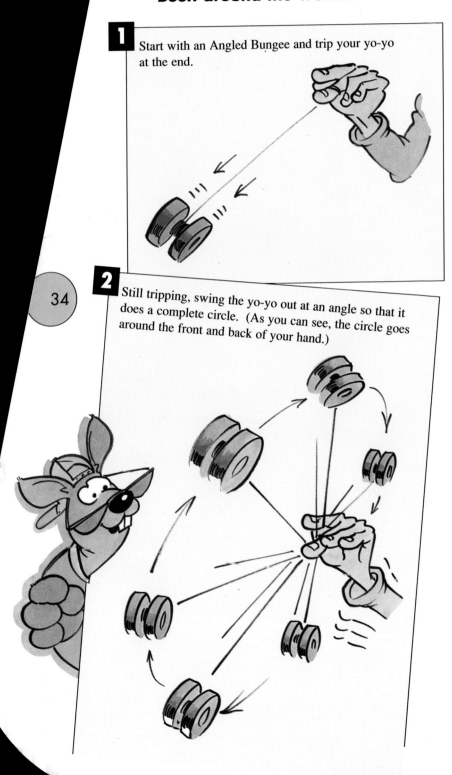

THE
BABY

5 Bring your free hand down below the yo-yo.

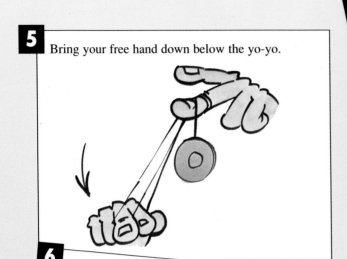

6 Spread the thumb and first finger of your free hand so that you make a triangle with this string.

7 The yo-yo should be in the middle of the triangle, and you can now make it rock.

If you've done the trick, you've probably found that it was pretty easy. So why is it here with the difficult ones?

Well, there's just one small point I forgot to mention.

Not only should the yo-yo rock, it also has to spin. In other words, you have to keep it tripping the entire time!

GOOD LUCK!

Take my word for it. This trick is difficult.

How difficult? Well, imagine trying to suck a football through a garden hose. That's about how difficult it is. So take my advice: leave this one alone until you can do all the other tricks.

The idea is to make the yo-yo do loops in the shape of a clover leaf. Here's how....

1 Start with an Angled Bungee. Flip it out in any of the three directions shown.

40

2 As the yo-yo comes back, send it over your wrist and back out in the next direction.

YO-YO

EXERCISE 1

Do Bungees while running on the spot. This will...

A Develop your coordination.

B Develop your leg muscles.

And, who knows...perhaps the yo-yo will replace the baton in the Olympic relay event!

EXERCISE 2

Do a Bungee.

Now, bending from the knees, go up and down in time with the yo-yo.
You can make it more fun by doing it to music – like they do on exercise videos. Come to think of it, I might produce my own. Mad Jack Yo-yobics!

IMPOSSIBLE TRICKS

You can do a Bungee straight down – now do one straight up in the air!

SEVERE HEADACHE WARNING!

Before doing this trick, please get a hard hat.
You can use the yo-yo with your hand...now try it with your foot!

1 Sit on a table.

2 Tie the loop around your toe – any toe will do.

3 Now do a Bungee.

Once you've mastered the "Toe Bungee," you can go on to do other toe tricks like "Around the World," "Rock the Baby," and "Three-Leaf Clover"...maybe!

SEVERE ODOR WARNING

If you're going to show off to your friends, make sure that you've washed your feet.

EVER GO SWIMMING?

Next time you're standing in the shallow end of the pool, try doing a few yo-yo tricks under the water! But this is getting silly. Time to let you invent your own tricks, I think –

SEE-YA!